SHEARSMAN

139 & 140

SPRING / SUMMER 2024

EDITOR
TONY FRAZER

Shearsman magazine is published in the United Kingdom by
Shearsman Books Ltd
P.O. Box 4239
Swindon
SN3 9FL

Registered office: 30–31 St James Place, Mangotsfield, Bristol BS16 9JB
(this address not for correspondence)

www.shearsman.com

ISBN 978-1-84861-924-1
ISSN 0260-8049

Subscriptions and single copies

Current subscriptions – covering two double-issues, each around 100 pages in length –
cost £17 for delivery to UK addresses, £24 for the rest of Europe (including the Republic
of Ireland), £28 for Asia & North America, and £30 for Australia, New Zealand and
Singapore. Longer subscriptions may be had for a pro-rata higher payment. Purchasers
in North America and Australia will find that buying single copies from online retailers
there will be cheaper than subscribing, especially following recent drastic price-rises for
international mail. This is because copies are printed locally to meet such orders from
online retailers. Due to the changes in 2021 regarding the treatment of low-value cross-
border transactions in the EU, purchasers in the EU (except for those in Ireland) are
recommended to use EU-based online retailers, although these can sometimes be a little
slow to update their databases for non-domestic publications.

Back issues from n⁰ 63 onwards (uniform with this issue) cost £9.95 / $17 through retail
outlets. Single copies can be ordered for £9.95 direct from the press, post-free within the
UK, through the Shearsman Books online store, or from bookshops. Contact us regarding
earlier issues (i.e. nos. 1–62), whether for single copies or a complete run.

Submissions

Shearsman operates a submissions-window system, whereby submissions may only be made
during the months of March and September, when selections are made for the October and
April issues, respectively. Submissions may be sent by mail or email, but email attachments
are only accepted in PDF form; submissions may also be made through the upload portal
on the Shearsman website (on the *Contact* page). We aim to respond within 3 months of the
window's closure, although we do sometimes take a little longer.

This issue has been set in Arno Pro, with titling in Argumentum. The flyleaf is set in Trend Sans.

Contents

After the Pruning

to sit down
        on cedarwood bench,
on flower

           craftsmanship
        with patience

is *virtu*
quoth the Roman

        on
radio waves

he said are you
listening

        the daily tasks
laid out
take that branch

        "un nuage
           plus grand
que la montagne"

about to flower

        * * *

observe
as it is about to flower
as it divides into four equal parts
that strive equally
and the stem or stalk also

          up-
                    wards
while in Giotto's painting
          the angel
dives down
                    the background
a "heavenly" blue

                    * * *

sticky leaves
                    in Spring

the pending blossoms
weigh heavily

          I have tied
a string to the lamp
which hangs
from the ceiling

"la fleur est la raison
la raison est le sexe"

                    * * *

later,
           at the farm

three dogs
will leave no footprints

Mouchette, Fleurette,
Apache
will be remembered
in the child's mind

                    and the pigeons
coo, coo   woo again

caw, caw ... flies by
                    mocking
they walk up and
down the field

                * * *

looking for a piece of wire
to keep the cat off the roof
killed seven, the newborn
pigeon's
           wings
shaking in the light
in the morning light
                the flower
not yet

           fully open

                * * *

"gauzy"

Ida Rubinstein
didn't like to have her picture taken

in Giotto's painting
not a leaf that stirs

and Joseph is dreaming

"why should I move
from this place"

                              where are you?

            I'm bundled up
in permafrost
            turning *au ralenti*

                  * * *

then tell,
            tell us
Mister Jo
the cost of dreams
their dimensions in space
the inscriptions on rock face

                  one sees
      stars

"le ciel"
the sky

the sky is like a painter's house
when his pictures

        "seine Bilder

sind auf-
gestellet"

       * * *

        up /
      down
as in a musical score

         anyone there, is
        anyone there
        turning the page

left hand, left hand
by heart, by heart

when he died, he left
no "image filmée, pas le moindre
enregistrement de sa voix"

            (Ravel)

       * * *

on the top shelf
    the 'City of God'
we toured

Dardanus
walked with his crowd

later,
the 'written stone'

we found
occasionally
four in the clover

Oh happy days!

* * *

but
    now,

in the tapestry of the moon

"les pétales froissés
baignant dans un lac de sang"

suddenly at full display

towers
we made
        of air
unscrolled, and wings
                (to soar)

to walk on snow

through summer

Jill Jones

The Nights Before Your Return

it wasn't what I intended for year's end —
to come home in pre-dawn light — traffic was scarce
— I know I'd stayed too long, taking measure
of myself

— the sky's still overcast — I drank too much —
I've done worse —

I have no resolutions now and never have — the city
was layered in smoke, skirted by bats, filled with glittery
colours — little 'saturns', clever arrangements
of light — still the childlike wonder

the streets moved in groups — dogs still barked, cats
still hid — a day to be faced with or without explanation

in the morning — what does a 'good time' mean?
— a way of being that ends up trashy, but not
ill, remorseful, bereft

*

she leaves me a breathy message — I imagine touching
her — I take my phone outside to the wooden table
— we discuss the future of the euro, a friend's job
states of art and nation

then I'm alone with the meditation on self — to go
beyond self, rediscover effort

*

sun shines down on King Street — awnings angle
on the footpath into shadows — news of drownings
terrorism, sport sport sport — the street's full of couples

getting used to being alone for a while — crying
in the health food shop between echinacea and
St John's Wort — do tears smell? — internal
aromatherapy?

shopping shopping, everyone's shopping in
sales time, but I don't buy much — the bus squeaks by

*

the fan is spinning — work at the screen done — a cricket
in the garden — a goods train's metal clanks, blades
of the fan pulse false waves of air —

here's me alone (ah, poor me!) and tonight everyone is
door door, swinging jokes and words between fences —
I'm nowhere in this, bemused by that

I drink my tea's silence — air is noise, songs on
different waves, but the same window

I've finished reading someone's memoir and
I don't care — its anecdotes drift without punchlines
or reasons — on TV, What's Eating Gilbert Grape?
very touching

we win the Fifth Test, a wind's blowing through the house
taking some of the heat out — the Australian Open is
coming soon — to the south-east lights probe the sky

*

I'm back at work — today was a planning day — sourness
near the surface — outside a glare of summer slackness

tonight, a play about Oscar Wilde, not such a great play —
The Judas Kiss — first half too expository — don't
we know all this?! — second half more affecting — I felt
attuned then to the Oscar-like sentiments — Naples
— older than *inglesie* — Naples of sun, volcano
and the melancholy bay Shelley brooded over — what
we can't lie about, Oscar could lie about — ... and
that's the Irish for you, our Irish friend says...
— ...OK?

if it's about love, how can we love these days in the face
of social eavesdropping, breathless advice? — where is
the bright room, beside the bay? — sun wakes you
the moon's tide draws you to the body, hand and skin
— this is all that's left after the money goes, the
reputation — the skin expands

but tonight there's fun for afterwards — cheap
champagne — cheap matches that don't light — now
I am falling asleep, and love creeps up on me — her
postcard of a turtle — she's sick and I worry but I must
sleep — alone with the fan —

*

free tickets again in the heat, is this how to live? — song
of the circus — du soleil — girls together on a trapeze
a frisson — it's about skill and trust — rehearsed
rehearsed rehearsed — a woman's voice hangs over
the stage —another language, no words to ground
my mind — the mind has to make itself up — love
must enter the mind, bring together the whole
— figures of air invite further mysteries

too tired for late dinner — I must be dreaming of
the sky again, how it wants me to escape — but
escape what, to where

*

green tea floats — silence or melancholic music? —
there's nothing heavy in the air tonight — no cars
or doof doof or bad mouths, only echoes, tremolos
in a small corner of the vastness — or just my mind in
its argument with my forgetfulness — my attempt
to shut out death, of something

— next door hoses while we all wait for rain — noise
of the fan is this room's own summer sea — the planes
are using a different flight path — she says she'll be
home soon, the trip has been too much

*

down by the harbour this evening, B tells me how hard
is marriage, his children learning another language
— and poetry? — he suggests Pessoa, Machado
Andrade, Amichai, Bachri — yes, no women

the sky is purple, clouds are tipped orange — the air
is cool and dry, stone steps hugged by weeds —

D takes our pictures on the steps, she's leaning
on a brick wall to get the angle — the city and its dark
waters glide close by — for half an hour after I see
purple then orange squares

it makes fire in everything I touch —

Hungers and Sacrifices

We uncurl, brazened by the yard sun.
    The day's peppy. We clown around bushes where you
retrieve a broken cup, a trace of magenta at the lip.

In the affable light your forehead's glowing.
Your blue eyes turn sapphire in the angle of sun.
    Mine green like a wall.

A wind gust tackles our cheeks, we attempt affinities
with morning's jazzy ions, the horizon's pastels.

We applaud freshness, day's breath streams through
    our hair, clothes we've lowered onto our silent skins.

The drain next-door gurgles again.
    There's the woof of a washing machine.
We raise bare forearms to demolish intrusion.

Tea leaves gather at the edges of cups, tired
    blood-brown lots in backwash.

We continue our speculations about the lightness
    of midday among a crinkly circus of vegetable beds
a trough of compost, the legato of decomposure.

I spot an old doll in a basket, its cracked right cornea
    victim of childhood games. Though it may be
sacrificial, its chipped red fingernails are still happy.

A discreet but rickety feeling is unleashed by afternoon's
    indolent light, beside the music of a table cloth.

We waver like cellophane in evening air, under the pale
    gold surface of the moon.

We feel like conspiring, stealing our identities to become
useless celebrities, stoic detectives, immaculate drama queens
    or better still, mechanics in love.

We drive at midnight down the dirt track to the weir.
There's an awkwardness when we stop
    then kindness enters with its unconditional moment.

We remember what we first touched together
what each day has done and undone
    and what's washed away.

A Warning at the Table

We get the monster we pay for.
It will finish each day like another meal.
The table is ordinary but wide.

Even in the dust
I told my monster there was more.
Come on, the bread, the beer, the apple, the tea!

Here are the crumbs that follow us.
They dance at doors, with the serious money
and the children who warn us.
What they find under the table.

Every door has its monster.
Every monster once was a child.

Alex Wong

Breakers

1

Dear, though you happened to
Me, and I'm
So many pieces (still enough alive)
Of the old—the very young—thing you met

While time was hanging pleasures out
Ornamentally, almost, over want;

And you have leave to read again
Those passages; perhaps keep easy
Ridicule at your side, your beck,
And speculate with a rending retrospect…

Friend, how I think I felt, and how I feel
The good of it,
          the frame in which were set
Those new joys over enjoyment, still
Flashing out
          in the corner shades of mind.

And so I push myself
Back to original pleasure, and through that
To uncertain knowledge. Another kind
          of 'suffering-into-wisdom'?

Contact: never then mistook itself,
Even going out and going out.

2

To be creature wanted utterly,
Felt into being body.

A little talk,
        maybe a short
Zip; your things in crumple;

And you would push
        behind seduction this
Feeling inside itself.

3

A single blind delicious wish
                went offering to be met:
Come out, alongside,
            inside, anywhere...
The bare encounter made itself a zone.

And life would bend together in a
            steep delighted liking;

Glad in hard affection, found
A breakneck tenderness
            I'd never known.

4

So it drove down deeply into pleasure,
Spitting out awful power into the night—

Engine of nerve and mind. your exigent Orphic
Force (corroborating such of mine
As poured out, drawn, from sets and lairs)

Pulling us in
        to a new commotion: power

Given off wordlessly in the fine, lost silence
Broken
        in music of
        various flattering wants:
As though the last moment ever said and said
Do you like getting loved?

To love
        like being meant:
        colossally.
Generous beyond measure / arrogant.
You could see to me with unruly understanding,
Take us in hand,
        held into a subtle collapse.

5

That broad, unroaring, sane imbalance broke
Hard,
        driving
        in vague demand
Over the many-pointed voluptuarism
Down
        beneath your pleasures' surfaces:

Submarine finger cities, all
Cavernous habitats, the woods of horns:

A glad, flirtatious half-destructiveness,
Not rounded—whetted only sharper still
In the swell
        it raked
        with a dexterous art of sense.—

Your deeply fucking landscape
     cut
The gathered power more and more intense.—

The peaks amounted, broke:
               broken, embraced
In loving wash the warm solidity,

     Showing in the contours of the face,
     Spreading over the ranges; getting lost;

Searching for the scene of your met self
(Withheld) and mine in meeting—
               and withdrew.

The strong remembered riptide
     of that new-discovered coast.

6

Do you think I'm getting almost Californian?
Happily expansive about feelings
Without being rude, supercritical or feline?

That edge. To understand it would be much.
Between the impossible not made possible
And happily unmanageable love.

Katy Evans-Bush

Opportunity

What a wonderful world we live in
every morning a new chance

This morning I woke up in my bed
left the warm bed
slipped slippers on and then made tea

Got to boil the kettle even though I can't
have the heating on
got to open a canister
and put the leaves
into my sweet teapot and got to pour

freshly boiling water over the tea
so that it blossomed

and then I got to pour tea into
my blue & white charity shop mug,
milk in first, of course
because I'm only a philistine

and then the tea
the delicate, astringent tea
from which a small plume of steam
rose in the freezing kitchen

Resolution Bingo

You're not having so much luck with the multiple choice:
Who has that much room to manoeuvre?
It's the start of the year and everyone is pretending
it's a blank slate and they all have options.
Choose which bill to pay:
A: electric
B: food
C: piper

No, seriously, what's your resolution? It's a new year,
they keep saying that. And don't say pilates.
Here's a graph of common resolutions,
what percentage of each age group had chosen which
from the New Year's Resolution bingo card.

Looking out your window you see the same
old chimney pots. The same old broken-looking aerials
and the top of the big tree over in the town car park,
behind a roof, swaying hard in a high wind, with a few
seed pods and leaves still clinging to its high branches.

The Tightrope

It's the tightrope you can have a cup of tea on
— preposterous tea tray balancing, wobbling
only with the wire, as the wire wobbles, the way
a tall building sways with the movement of the air,
of the planet. You're alone up here, you're an astronaut,
but the crowd — these earthflubbers are somehow
your people. They stand and gape at you in your element,
they siphon you, your tea tray, into their eyes, into their
souls.

They can't pull you. Here you are. You take a sip. Ahhh.
You sip again. They gasp and you extend a little finger.
You're just showing off now with your cup of tea
and you know how many people as calm, as skilled,
as agile and balanced as you have fallen to their deaths.
But what of it? What of it? What of it?

Claire Crowther

Hazards and Thrown Humans

Whatever material you might consist of:
I'm wood.
If I pillowed my top layer—material
having a skin,
beneath it electrons are going and coming—
I'd soften
my surface, my tegument, down my flights—past
these hard pillars
that turn me and twist me—I could become twill.
I could bolster
the humans thrown down me, they would not break.
Window,
you melt, you transition—your glass, glass can hold it,
a body,
glass can flush back across opened space as a body
is hurled,
the thrown human will raise your resistance. A flash
of glaze holds
and the flesh does not shatter. And you, iron fence:
you cry 'Hazard!!!'
to passers-by. Guard rail, you can stop them, humans.
Persist.
Don't deny your ideals are forged out of you, beaten:
you're fixed
at three feet, but, young pickets, you quiver, you judder,
you shudder,
you shake and you tremble excited! You'll bolt past
a spine,
an upside-down head. Up you go. Then when bone
and dear blood

slam at you, they'll meet metal sky. Why so thoughtless
sweet matter?
Humans will lob fling and sling their own species away,
catapult
sisters and brothers. Inertia is not so supine
as it's strong.
We must learn to desist, then, materials: matter
does mind.

Covert Bird

Out, I walk miles through fields to find the quail
where it calls
its doubled syllables: *where where   wit wit*

I've left my shy writer in our stone home.
She's shackled.
She's a pinioned creature: *there there   sit sit*

Our stones clutch air with swollen thumbs. Sick of
cracked tarmac,
cold and teary, I turn: *scare scare   quit quit*

Back, limp room to room. Which is she locked in?
Fly, quail, flush
up from your obscure run: *where where   wit wit*

Word Hurt

Words
drill walls
along my street.

Jolt
my brain
hips, knees, skull, feet.

Pain
builds thought
to break it. Verbs

dig
the road
and bulldoze kerbs.

Would-
worlds lay
infinitives,

make
tarmac
who-sensitive,

pierce
my gate,
gouge my flagstones.

Mind
has tools
and mends alone.

In The Memory, The Face Is Stored With Chemicals And Those Chemically-induced Associations Can Be Shaken Up, By A Blow To The Head Say, And Lost For A While Until You Look At Me

I
want that needle in the brain
that says 'again'.

Meeting regularly, I was grateful that they had dyed their hair red. I could look for that sign in the crowds coming up from the underground. I could guess it was their face or at least make only the occasional mistake. I could construct from red.

'I said hello in Cheap Street,'
my old friend said. 'Then you—
you didn't say hello.
It wasn't really you.'

I have a common face
and that was what they saw—
and, I would say, that that
was also who they saw.

When I've been lying in the palm of your hand, my cheek against your thumb, cortisol rises, I jump and my face heads up five feet to see yours.

Sophia Nugent-Siegal

Flotsam and Jetsam

I—Shipwreck

In the union of the tongue
Coming together and apart are one
The marriage of the sword

Cloven-footed beasts
Like the queen of Sheba
Mistaking a mirror for water

The river begins in the broken word
It becomes Narcissus' reflection
It becomes Echo's echo

Her yearning is all voice
Her voice empty of meaning
Like a cracked cup

II—Disguise

Masked in the sea
The spirits rise
Drunk on themselves

To their own selves
Turned in
Like fugitives   or careless coats

The label on the outside
Does not scratch the skin

It is the aureole of Europa
A cloth halo bellied up with salt-wind
Above the hunched back of the bull

The god in meat
Wrapped about the eye
Like a snake
Or a snake-skin washed ashore
A shadow in the sands

III—Quest

We seek to know
But do we know to seek?

In the labyrinth there are no doors
But at its centre Rosamund

What sort of rose is she?
To the philosopher a crystalline sphere
An elemental testament to triangles
To the bishop's ear a mermaid's song
Communing each upon the sharpest rocks
But to the fearful and the weak
The rose smells sweet

IV—Recognition

They try the test of mirrors
To see if a creature knows itself
But does a thing ever see itself in mirrors?

Or rather the surface
Like the moon whose craters need telescopes

Stroked by the poets for centuries with goose-quills
And trapped in nets of numbers by the sages

The acrobatics of vision
Bring sight tumbling to the mind
Blocks rolled downhill

It is the patterns written on sand and water which last
What Electra remembered was a curve
And that was how she knew

V—Conspiracy

The suspiration of conspiring breaths
Breeds the spirits between the mouths
The immaterial substances of angel wing and demon foot

Weaving a web like a spider which bites mouths alone
Mandibles clacking out skeins
Like scissors striking aetherial skin

And then Arachne gone
With her Velázquez spinners
Replaced by factories of water and fire
(The new dispensation)

It is from these innards
It is from these inwards parts
Needles that swim like tadpoles through the weft
Combine and strike flame
Devouring the cotton air
And the slave's hand

Speaking of Caesar

VI—Strike

The cessation and the blow
A work stoppage perhaps of the breath
That is what it all tends to
This gardening of care
This plot to tend

The stem bleeds when cut
A nymph's torso it might be
Running from a God's hand
In this stillness
Pointing and growing at the sun
In accusation of life

VII—Rough Music

There is nothing speaks so loud as a wound
The scarlet monarchy of silence deafens
And, like the painter, we wrap ourselves up in our own night terrors

In the shadows we shrink back
Which are really blue
Like bruises

The wolf will come and puff down
The house of shadow
For you could only build it in the light

Such opacity! Daedalus sets jewels
In blind sockets
And makes a living idol

Stone hands are, you see, washed white

VIII—The Empty Stage

At last come to the landing stage
They play dead
Chalk on black
They bathe in flatness
And the flatness must be bathed

The vinegar sponge on Calvary
And the rest is bitterness!
The appeal lost amidst the confusion of tongues
And a burial amidst sweetness!

Borne on the tide the player prince
Viking amidst his licking dreams

And after the last line is cast
        Like a lure cast into water
Nothing but ripple and rumour

Jack Barron

Silent Reading

Almost angelic the arc, flutter
　　then wow: blank face, its winged
talk in some unquietness
　　turns dark, late work to utter

what soon withdrew, in love
　　with slighter matter. The living
room against the language game,
　　the facts just shy of

consummation in the darknesses:
　　they wound, as you
go without saying. In the head
　　does dawn appeal, loose as

pooling water, unanswerable
　　breathless stuff spilt
across the slim volume, which,
　　just briefly, you're able

to feel, like velvet or something
　　floral: a more denied
desire it fits as in a page
　　the dawning plaint for want

of unbelief. I know I read
　　just by fainter light to form
a fine excess and listen for
　　you. It's how the simple span

is tried again, the tear once more
    illapsing into paper; I hear
by this a music out of true
    about what this is speaking to.

In So Far As

Pressed flower: we play in softlock,   an ending
in itself,   so far   as the pressure will allow.
Each stone is precious, and not to us unconscious,

is made in the graphic's fault; is that
at which we knelt, read yew and litanies, wept
    and always rose again.

It is as we may think it: names left
    like dark patterns becoming pathways
       purposed for our being

in the substance that appals us: the firelit dead
among the dead, the prime example
uncertain when close-to. For there is death

in every loop: *Pressed flower*, its inisolable
loss   lies flattered, so racked with joy
    and some more burning voice. By which

within so many turns   to rise   is our pain
refreshed,   an even breeze against all
    doubt.   I say pain, I mean it as an end.

Archaeopteryx

As you walk the jaded candour
of twilit playing-fields, something less
    is understood: a passing hour,

its different pause and paraphrase,
come as though an afterlife
    has taken place. As one, in a day's

indelicate extent, may wince
beside the changing-rooms to touch
    the bricks long-since

retouched like minds irreconciled;
or else recall the scaffolding,
    once intimating shadows on the grass,

now struck. And fear, in its wild
registrations of remembrance,
    plays a part across the cooling world

where you mortalise oblivion
with belief, where that weird limit,
    your fealty to it, seem so alien

and just as if you stand
about a massless transept
    thinking of glancing south, and

do, to where stray echoes flare
in ashlar-dust and sun recrests itself
    all difficultly bright. Here

it is the same: you nerve in tracery
a pitch's stranger lay
    and gather other means to phrase

the harmony's dissent, its reticence,
and catch your finger on a twig
 as you confess: there was no elegy.

For that, for now, so far as it goes,
is what is true and catastrophic,
 that which falters in the welt of shades

stepping along the awkward line
chalked subject to the earth
 and up towards the beck. Imagine

it instead, *The Death
of the Virgin*: how she rests; the window
 being left there, meaning death;

how it creates the loss, crosses
time and time again; the tempera's
 blank through which we pass

with tragic frequency or dear refrain
an unbecoming look
 and murmur of design.

Such labour fits remains
as much as suffering—the flinch sleeps,
 leaving each to each at pains

to bear indifference as just
that: craquelure and birdless air above
 her finer skin, so like a solid thing

Joseph Nutman

Aubade for the one who walks with me
After Juan Ramón Jiménez

I meet them at the high place—out of town upon the hill,
I hear their footsteps in my slowly waking thoughts,

and then, there—as I come out of the woods
in the sun—*here you are*—in step at my shoulder,

always in sync as soon as we meet again, like old friends
who pick up the thread and never miss a beat.

Occasionally, I catch them moving like me—except—
how they glide through space seems much more elegant,

though I'm slightly older, more bold and less sombre,
so I take first turn to describe the scene with language:

chalk hills rolling eastward, woods (probably private),
poplars on the horizon, and the cresting morning sun.

My walking partner waits, shakes their head, corrects me,
murmurs artfully about what's actually arrayed—

> *hunched shoulders of iron pyrite dusted with sugar,*
> *an arborescent moot of elders caught by lithograph,*
> *a row of field hands regard the long day's work ahead,*
> *a pantheon of gods in an incandescent aperture.*

I humour them—nod, and do my duty as the scribe,
but whose words are likely to stay standing
when I die?

Pine

The crematorium was packed from pew to rafters—
a homage to the way he touched so many in his life
and the fact his life ended at least fifty years too early,
your circle grand and sweeping
when you're young.

The celebrant invited the brimming room to come,
approach the coffin now and say your farewells—
a spell that froze all in attendance for a spell,
a hard equation asked of the class—
no raised hands.

I took that snug and thorny opening,
thirty paces never felt so long,
all those eyes upon my back—
no one told me to take my tongue,
or what would be appropriate right now.

What's the etiquette?
My right hand felt foreign to my body
placed upon the casket lid.
I wanted to set the bar in my life but not like this,
inadequate—I made my retreat.

A score of years and unfinished business,
grief ages like whisky—bide time before a sip,
now I'm as ready as I will ever be
to dust off this memory,
my palm upon its lid.

Glasshouse

Thick air caught in your throat
sets you coughing. Water vapour

condensing on glass, mould
creeping over the windowsills.

Blow-flies, crane-flies
—a richness of corpses.

Cereus, beacarnea,
neoregelia—

this place belongs to those
who can suck nutrition out of the air,

can trap water
in spiked cup, swollen foot.

Blunt snouts pushing up,
broad tongues, pink at the tips

as though touched, enflamed
—you recognise a language here,

silent, shared, like the glances
girls exchanged in the mirrors

back at school, tiniest flicker
of lip or eyebrow heavy with significance

—a whole coded repertoire
and you shut out, burning to know.

Priest

John Singer Sargent, *Vespers*, 1909

This time, you see it.
Something in the shape of the face,
the dark short pointed beard.
A face from a snapshot,
a small blurred photograph
deep in your mind.

He doesn't smile.
He doesn't move a muscle.
He is as much a part of this place
as the stone pillars,
the whitewashed walls.
As the five worn stone steps
leading into the dark,
which is where you must go.

He doesn't try to hide the truth
but he gives you this cloister,
this soft settling evening dusk
for as long as you need it.

Not forgiveness you've come here for
but compassion. To learn
how it might have been.

Standing Water

J.M.W. Turner, *Landscape*,
oil on canvas, painted about 1840

A place seen from a train window
—marshland? water-meadow?

Perhaps a river, overflooded in winter,
drowning its banks.

Standing water, bruise colour
—the way blood pools.

Sodden remains of a small fire.
Ruins of a day.

Plant bodies, peat layer—
start of the process of breaking down.

Winged form? Mist rising,
shadow projected on thickened air.

Ghost of a boat,
half its own burial

boatman long gone
& this place unbecome.

In Winter

In winter, you track him,
following the spoor of his thought.
Smudge in the snow, broken back
of a spent match. He plays out his mind
like a fishing-line, desperate
for something to catch.

The forest smells him, makes itself quiet.
Vicious, he picks up a fallen branch.
Thwock of wood on living wood,
snap of wings—some bird taking flight.
Quick hiss of his cigarette-end
as it hits the snow, sparks out.

All winter, he walks the paths
and you walk with him. You drag
on his cigarette, the Schnapps from his flask
burns your throat. But the crystals that hang
in the freezing air are only his breath,
only his steps leave prints in the snow.

Does he sense it? His mind, your mind,
reaching out like fingertips—
Sometimes he stops, cocks his head
like a dog, listening—to what,
you can't know. He trips, swears,
goes on. And you follow.

Leia K. Bradley

No One's Penelope

Trusting stability takes habit, Martine, I know.
You resent my need to find beauty in every leaf that falls into my path. Look,
this one matches my lipstick, crimson as a stolen kiss. You roll your eyes
at the messages I read from a Morse-flickering streetlamp;
you think I am frivolous, maybe, that I should be more like you: ready
as an adder. Poised to strike, to sink fast your fangs
into an inevitable enemy. Do you jump, ever, at your own reflection in a
                                                    [looking glass?

All the lapis lazuli in the world cannot protect you
from your high roil of fear. Preparedness against pain
is a soldier's causeless life, and a short one at that. Look,
I don't know if I want there to be a happily ever after
more than I want to know if it is worth sacrificing myself
to hold your Ship of Theseus mind together. I am
no great seamstress or healer. Yes, I know the words and ways
to enact a great love, to tie myself to its sails and sing my own siren psalm
to keep the bloom ever verdant, but I do not know
how to make someone let me.

I have valerian for sweet, lulling calm, Saint John's Wort
for heart healing, feverfew for when your mind swells
with rage so incandescent I fear
your skin will crack open like a vase in an opera house, that
white-hot light will gush and pour from you
in a heavenly, righteous burn, all
heat, all saviorhood, all abominable depths of care. What of your own stake
in your own serenity? Odysseus pretended to be mad purely so
he did not have to play
clever hero once again. Lost to his own tragedian need to outwit,

you, too, will have no one to return to if you choose to sacrifice yourself. You
will only be alone.

I want to hold you, but you shrug me away from the armor of your skin,
and I don't know how much longer, Martine, I can be strong enough to stay
while you choose a hero's journey, as if we all don't know
about Sebastian's arrows and Lucy's eyes,
how saints become saints, how witches become immortal.
You do not need to burn and I am no Penelope.

Dirty Deaths in a Gin-Clean Year

What waif of an afternoon wisps shut
    to herald heaving storms—
lion or lamb or lovechild,
    it's supposed to be the beginning
of something that glows.

But the sky shudders, shuts its blue doors,
    cirrus hinges whining—
the wrong ripples of time stop short,
    gnarled roots and nameless dew and gardenias
guessing at gods.

Lithe lily-capped nymphs lilt maleficence
    beneath storm-spring eves, and
I turn my umbrella upside down,
    hope to drink someone else's first chapter—
maybe the devil's or maybe mine, but

lately, I lead the foals to the field,
    just hoping for a rodeo of redos
looping lassos around what it means to love whiskey that bites,
    and women that bite harder, whistling
like any Hank or Johnny croon—

not too far from a far cry,
      but the willow's got to weep for somebody.
The dear and the dearly parted
      thumb old wallows on the five string,
lull low the ins and outs of the in between,

twirl me round in the tall grass to the bluegrass.
      This is the jump and jive from the Other Side,
from this springtime of teeth and bent knees
      The earth and I got dirty deaths in common, so
I put my spine to the dirt and promise not to leave.

Mark Fiddes

Interior with young woman seen from behind
(After Vilhelm Hammershøi)

A Delft tureen, the artist's wife
turned towards the lilac wall.
Their faint blue symmetry.
A stillness created not by paint
but what is beyond the window
across the courtyard in the stalls
where they are flaying a deer,
drinking aquavit, slapping backs
and singing bawdy songs.
Blood pools under the carcass.
Late flies cluster on the new pelt.
Along a forest path, leaves stir
with long-departed footsteps.
Smoke rises from the valley.
By the lake, urgent lovers kiss
under clouds pressing south
where a boy king is crowned.
Factories smelt shining miracles.
Ships load with dark cargoes.
A city falls to a bored army
behind hungry, unruly canons.
A century of noise commences
the way it means to go on.
Yet this day is framed by Ida,
a still life caught in his interior,
the back of her neck, her hair
unbraiding before a lilac wall,
sparking a million revolutions.

(High) Anglicanism

Death arrives layered in a more flattering black
for High Anglican funerals like this.

Death distributes roses in original skin tones
with unforgiving pins.

Death pumps our lungs like tiny pipe organs
between our hearts and whatever's left outside.

Death throws out handfuls of motes to float
like bridal veils in flat sunlight.

Death watches us through Gucci glasses darkly
from the rocky pulpit taking notes.

Death flirts over the orders of service and slips
naked between the psalter's pages.

Death prefers a kneeling position
for which embroidered hassocks are provided.

Death traces all the former lovers' names
in serifs on plaques and sinking flagstones.

Death awaits the next booking as we leave,
prim as a lily, scented with naphthalene.

Newfoundland

How this year's seasons hurry past each other
as if wanting the whole decade done with.
The sky is wiped clean like a cheap tablecloth.
Each day away is snatched away
before you have finished with it.
Props are being dropped in the background.
Orders are shouted. Vans reverse.
You know that one day all this will be different.
Even the yellow leaves will have gone
so you order another glass though you shouldn't.
No one can refuse you that.
You get to your feet and start to dance
with the soft musculature of the air.
You smell the exquisite resin on its neck.
You hold its every pause and you feather step.
That old witchcraft down your spine
forgiving your feet now clumsier in the dusk.
Here is the orchestra you asked for.
The crooner with broken eyes in a white tux.
The stars are out, one for everyone you knew,
including ours by which we found our North.
Beneath it, our delicious, catastrophic meltdown.
Ah. Here comes the ubiquitous accordion.
Someone wants a tip.

David Miller

Path

the stain
lifted itself

& flew
& then collapsed

stain or shadow

**

garden table
garden chair

white chair
white table

she would smoke a small cigar
& gaze & think & meditate

the bougainvillea's no more
the eucalyptus tree tall

**

the sheet music shop yielded unexpected treasures

but then it was gone
abandoned & boarded up

just dirt & rubble where it stood
the corner restaurant the same

the train station
disused

trams run there now

**

a swift flight
past the bushes

in the rain

which bird?
too quick to see

**

there's rain
& there's rain

there are dreams
& there are dreams

**

a gardener comes here unseen
you can see where he has worked with the plants

no there is no gardener
you can see that the weeds tell their own story

the philosopher rode into college on a horse

the horse absconded
greener pastures awaited

or gods

**

if a path / then a path

if a garden / then a garden

if a dream / then a dream

if the night / then darkness

**

my hand twists this way
twists that way

in one world I would raise an arm
in another I wouldn't

perhaps
perhaps not

**

letters painted on stones
on rocks on walls

individual letters
or in rows

all your rings necklaces bracelets

**

the shadow of a ladder
the shadow of someone climbing up a ladder

the shadow of someone climbing down
& then climbing up again

personal identity is much debated
& to little end

**

the shop where he worked
sold bric-a-brac & souvenirs

but there was dust & dirt everywhere

from demolition work
& death

's dirt & rubble

he was trained as an engineer
& as a film-maker

& he made films

but that's where he was
incongruously

we sat at cafés after hours
late into the night

street-walkers passed by
& transvestites

we drank wine & talked
& looked around

to no harm

**

the red admiral
opens & closes its wings

closes & opens its wings

on stone
stone on stone on stone

**

a long climb
up that iron staircase

how many flights?
spiral

& then flames

which ascend
& then descend

to a little above the head

& then ascend

**

the lamp?
there is no lamp

the door?
there is no door

the house?
there is no house

the path?
there is no path

**

blackbird
chiffchaff

robin
hedge sparrow

wren

not less
not more

only
with

***

Tom Cowin

On Ancestry

to the exfoliating dawn up
Fulking Scarp beside Perching
lost village whose calcifying

voices raise the pale fire grass
of morning. Curvatures
of impossible shelter, where

to rest but the hook of an arm,
wriggling comfort among
the chalkblindings and Devil's

Bit stillbursts. His limping
chafes at the skin of day
starting to cloud, deafening

Fasciated

An interior, a queue
and lit like deluge

I could so suggest
a mutual solar

low-level language
barrier is a beautiful

alterity and bur to
catch the way the day

tumbles through
the plate glass is

like an over-bloom
excess like below

the apron like petalling
the rounded glow

of possess flattens
reciprocal absorbency

like glutting anthers spark
broader than love

or leaf shapes
fully open to each,

foxgloves, forsythia, euphorbias, lilies,
and verbascums such as the mullein.

Sun Facing

Gridlocked all the way back
to the rising sun, clutch fluid issues

systemic drip pressures
peripheral nerve firing

a poorly pigmented
rind of morning.

Winter heliotrope glister listless
in winters almost spring, and I stop

seeing the leaden light
just the stalks becoming my sight,

defenceless cells left to float flicker
like the anxious pulse

in an eyelid across
the roadside chaos and I stop

seeing the sparkle and all
I can see is the clogging mineral

air and it glows like all
the world's heliotrope.

Raise face to its winter
flowering flecks,

all sorrow squeezed out cherry pie red
stone shrapnel would be such gentle

renting of the taut
and febrile moment.

Katherine Meehan

Riding the Gallows

Into the great cosmic blank you can enter your choice:
 Void or world. Choose both. Okay?
No one gives a fuck about transcendence.
One sees everywhere the terrible shame of turning away
 and binding oneself to like *super* deep thoughts.
 No one should want this.
Like a defamatory fresco slapped
 on the city walls, you are an act
of humiliation and treachery—
 simply by noting there is nothing fresh
in the moral woodland, the trees are ill-intentioned,
 they wear martyrs, each one a copy
of some other martyr, the genealogy
 of suffering, mass-produced and flimsy,
with no record of its origins except
 the ones we found in the fairy land
 death-in-life almost anticipated.
We are not sure if this is why
 when the lights go out, you are lit
head first by the implication
 that "mundus inversus" is
 the proper order of things, that only through
inverting oneself in tights and a jerkin
 can reality be properly perceived
and that it is dangerous to do so, there is
 a risk of stroke and asphyxiation—
the *actual* magician David Blaine
 righted himself once an hour
throughout his experiment with hanging
 to avoid brain damage and death;
it is likely that an early retirement,

taken in this fashion, would be less painful
than composing emails each day.

I Asked the Sky to Like, Subscribe, and Share

What if it was true, I asked myself, everything the sky said?
I was already inside of it; it spoke closely to me and everyone.
The sky—it sent me messages at night
I would stay awake for hours listening—
I spoke back to it, emptying myself—
no scrap of me got past it,
it had a way of turning me towards itself—
I asked if it would like to meet in real life;
I had no idea what that meant at least half the time.
I wanted to know it better—it did not have the trouble I had
with obsession; I wanted to get so near to it,
like Yves Klein leaping upwards in that picture,
only without the occulted tarp below.
Oh Void, love me insanely!

Another Poem About Death

After putrefaction
you will be identified
by your teeth.

Even the white horses who dance now in Vienna—the horse skeleton

is an open secret and
it will be an exciting
discovery one day.

Oh mom, oh dad, I have failed to be a daughter. I am consumed by regret.

In the most terrifying instance, the ego also
dissolves into a soup. It was life
we were afraid of, and

only Death has nothing to feel sorry for. The soil is alive;

we were put here to feed it.
They call this the *Great Work*:
composting the self.

From the rot in the mind, why is it so hard to act on love?

And it was love, I suppose, in the end—
my child, you are perishable
and so precious.

At one point I was going to Waitrose, receiving bare root roses in the post,

hoarding a series of black and white
snow days. I wanted so much
and I didn't want to give up anything else.

Between joy and ourselves there's only muscle and skin—

to reach the skull's semi-permanent
blank, pleasant expression
The absurdist plot

of this event reckons I am not much of a believer,

however much I desired it.
I used to like horseback riding too, but
it costs too much these days.

Rizwan Akhtar

shrink

dawn is like an unattended page
 squeaky birds tear complacency
gained over night in a warm quilt
"what was the dream that jolted"
you have asked me taking a note
images permuted scribbled
prophetic is so apocalyptic, the
silent is so noisy, in-between
I feared you declare me insane
or some other term unheard,
regime of physic disorders bigger
than a continent, wars say in
Africa plagued souls, Fanon lived
diagnosed the colonial madness
of establishing a collective dream
but a white dream with a white core
but my individual dreams are black
Lacanian, I cannot figure out like
Conrad's Marlow whether it is
a nightmare or not, 'You are my
shrink" 'you know history burns
jungles of community and when
we give vote we only think about
taxes', bloodshed is a parliament
we endorse—women in Kashmir,
Uyghurs in consternation facilities
Kurds in Armenia are not so distant
cousins of Bosnians and survivors
of Dresden and Palestine—all dreamt
freedom but then came Guantanamo
again we surrendered to the dreams

Of Blairs and Obamas, chucked out
Mandela installed Generals, democracy
is so subtle to the effect of a dream I am
narrating in which I saw a Syrian child
embraced by a Turkish solider and here
you are digging up its nitty gritty.

A Posthumous Letter to My Father

By writing this I am trying to make up
for not talking to you when the time
was ripe. Now the silence spooks
around your figure emerging from a
field of echoes seeing you hulking a
grey Vespa reaching home punctually—
regrets of my childhood climbed over
shoulders heavy despite that rare scowl
I caused by transgressing, that pretentious
despotism carried a child hidden inside,
a wispy odor of your sweat attended me
how you hatched vowels caressingly
and bred rebukes in manly plosives
on evenings I behaved and bothered
your lingual fits subsided benignly
couldn't a pathos be more handsome
than words held back long letting me
imagine a fossilized language breaking
rules of memory before I could close.

An Occasional Muse

"Let everyone know, I lived a very happy life."
—Orhan Pamuk

I saw you climbing the stairs on a day
when Lahore's winter gave a flimsy
knock making me descend silently
on words kept for the right occasion
outside cars cruised for parking dizzily
you came out of the one ejecting me,
silence with your plumose outfit wiped
off my heart, there was a premonition
that you are not a matrimonial type, a
perfect door for a stranger to settle in
without much ado feathering vanity.

Ghazal of Loss

An abrupt encounter revives loss
return to past also returns the loss

haven't I promised to be with you
doubting my words was also a loss

this ghazal's outcome is petrifying
moulded in English was Urdu's loss

for hours I mediated inside a shrine
a ritual of compensation of my loss

let's not show but seek anonymity,
lovers tend to hide; a scandal of loss!

a sadness looms over my couplets
Oh! melancholy the weight of loss

that random touch of your moist hands
that sweating body oppressed by its loss

now bombs not poems govern the city
our graveyards our oeuvres of new loss

in streets of Lahore I wandered with you
Love's Labour's Lost—added to life's loss

simple was the trap laid down by beloved
the poet freed with effort yielded to loss.

O, wilt thou leave me so unsatisfied?

The way you loved me was like a creeper hanging
on a rusty frame of a window creaking its history.
The way you left me was like a joke struggling to
find laughter and listeners are least histrionic.

On other occasions which can be called lyrical;
I encircled your vertebrate in search of the right
spasm but ended crawling over less aesthetic
outposts of flesh, a melancholic eye navigated
inspiration sinking when you referred to things
not worth mentioning making love—a tea-seller boy
singing a maudlin ditty choreographed by a pair of
lachrymose lovers, an audience for a happy ending—
so you wanted me to collect relics and acquisitions for
a museum not knowing who are curated and curators.

Bernadette McCarthy

The Sallies

One day, a woman gave him odd jobs.
He wanted to ask her what hellebores were
but could only say 'no' and 'fuck'.

She left him to the morning bee-drone.
The gutters were cleared of muck,
ivy tangled round pillars tugged down.

He was pulling up sallies everywhere.
The rotted clog of knotweed
he dug out from the rockery

was tough and rangy as a ram's hoof
and he felt vital again, like a rootball,
tracing the veins of it back to the pulse

of a shepherd in the Carpathians
hopping from one foot to the other
to stay the cold.

He eased buttercups out from under stones,
sweltering in the honey-glazed afternoon.
At five she gave him apple tart and tea,

which he had beneath the Pampas grass,
and a crisp brown note.
Going back, the drifting catkins

fleeced his shoulders like a *cojoc*
and the road was a river joining all rivers,
the Sullane, the Lee, the Danube.

The farmer's wife clattered down
from the tin roof to kiss him hello.
Where goats sleep is a good place to build a house

He went to gather kippeens—'small wood'
he muttered knowingly—
from the haggard and saw

that orchids were popping up like harlots
where he had dreamed April away.
He was grateful for the tropes of spring

as the trees told a rosary
in a tongue he no longer recalled,
responding to the breeze

as it wafted the willow down:
sally sáile
salix salcie

Pangaea

When you draw the blinds a wasp wakes up
a season too soon, bombing through our study
onto my knee. *A queen* you hiss, and I do not stir
though the satin of my pyjama leg is thin,
letting her rest so she will not sting;
each careless swipe easing the great dying
as the earth burns out for a centigrade.

While she strokes her maw I study your morning torso,
the Reeks and Appalachians a single spine
and wonder how the land split off like Adam's rib,
the beetles that smothered prelapsarian skies

petrifying where they dropped in the swamp.
My love, our bones may yet be coal
but for now we still have our continent.

The Arcanity of Pignut

Returning after the birth, I fear
that you will somehow slip off the garlic-lipped bank
into the brackish trout-meer;

should I teach you to stay safe—*get away, dirty*—
or should I initiate you in the alphabet
of swallows on a bleeding sky

or the aspirin musk of meadowsweet
that soothes those of a flighty disposition;
or the mystery of *fairy potatoes*—

how the stem runs straight as a stave
till the root veers off like a crozier's head
so that one must dig out its angle

with devotion to reveal the tuber?
Better, perhaps, I'd forget these woods,
teach you not to delve below

the muck shot through with weeds,
to disregard the call of bugle flowers
from the reservoir islands;

each flooded channel a trench
sullied by the struggle
of nature and knowing better?

Sylee Gore

Lastness

July dusk. Parched grass, pale whelk, sharp rock
Seaglass lump, maple lace, glazed cup, pine cone
Lichened twig, blunt cork, down feather, stubbed chalk
Moss, blackbird shell, acorn cap, quartz-stung stone

Talisman: the last word taught in childhood
Seed, stalk, husk—both archaic and brand-new
The first terms learnt in old age: will, heirloom
Legacy, testament; estate, accrue.

Winter morning. Cloud-white box, faïence tray
Plaster cube, salt cellar, tea sieve, brass latch
Beeswax taper, silk square, unfired clay
Alabaster urn, smoked glass, burnt match

This sun-ruffled catalogue, steadied by rhyme
This landscape of objects, shadowed by time

Voice

Apart is exquisite: one sun, one tower
one holy room paged full of days
yet dry, bare of form and steel power
The lone mind by the window lifts its gaze

Converge. Two voices strengthen thought, and ten
extend it. Plait the rope so taut it holds
apples, rings of roses, cobblestones, then
hoist beyond known doors. Court vertigo

The tower, extended, wants a chorus
not a mob. A tuning fork's tapped 'C' peals
the mind of fog to sound a ferrous
star: a bold north is the only way to see

Proud in splendour, yet waking life alone
a rooftop garden is the only home

I Prefer to Avoid Challenges

We use a list to wish. Stump of beeswax
in one brass cup, charred wick in the other.
Cars mimic waves, and the wires beneath things
distend and crack the clay to cuneiform.

We use a list to define: skyscraper
dive bar, summer on the chaise, belvedere
shivering chestnut-green in May.
In the round library, light soaring down

the page. Fingertip and thenar webspace.
Kneecap and lobe. A list helps us forget.
Overhead, separate clouds daub the eye.

We make a list to remember. Eyelash,
orbital bone, popliteal fossa,
the hollow at your throat, all the soft spots:
ripeness never fleeting before it's lost.

Ellen Harrold

The Carving Flint Rakes These Audios

Sweet, sooty cadmium floods the water bough, collapsing civilizations' dust through upended physics. The rate of replacement halts the surge, flickering o'er the supple weight cast by tidal bulge. The force has thus far obeyed number, although that may change. We have no empirical evidence that the laws of physics can't be broken. The judges usually just adjust them for any discrepancies. It's what makes humans so much more powerful than the universe: we can change our names.

There is a fishing hook caught in the shallows.

Dust floats dim and interesting amongst sweet-rot, coagulating. Or is it contaminating? There is a killer but no crime; more interest in judging the numbers.

Crushed Spine Split

Trawlers spark—
Star marked mirrors
hovering in supple care

Between
Arcs of grey/pink/blue

Converge at one with that great abyss.
At what fucking point does air fail to form sky?
When esophageal claustrophobia erupts
into limp fingers and sun-soaked lashes.

Taphonomies on Display

Ash fine mist catches on gallowed dew,
Laundering the sun stains on tin and cadmium glass
discarded.
Postmortem mornings for the turbulence of hierarchy
throwing downward
in the catchment area of free-form revels,
a fox lays its withered skull.
Old age having settled its chase.
Finalised in pale angles and caught breath,
a milky cloud saturating the eyes.

Pigmented light fulminates,
dying to soft reds, then pale grey.
Under the weight of commute drizzle,
some cyclists send their glances.
A pedestrian stops to stare.
Another calls the local council, snipping over the line
about rubbish
and needles in wait of wandering feet.

It takes two days for removal,
soft flesh begun its rot.
Lifted from that tarmac pitch
to ascend, a second coat of flames.

Ann Pelletier-Topping

Because her name ends in M

we drag her by the wrists
into the churchyard
among the headstones
she hardly resists

we scratch with feral claws
as if to snatch what's inside her
her face a flaming bloom
her arms tattooed in scrawls

pale blue eyes
plead with mine

but where does friendship lie
under a wounded sky

I long to fly between tribes
redraw the lines

out of myself
I am torn

a kestrel trembling
alone

Numerals

Coils of rope, bent fingers and lotuses
describe ancient numerals

though cuneiforms are more sexagesimal
and Hindu-Arabic more mathematical.

Numerals can be loud or quiet
but I prefer the loud Roman ones

screeched on a chest or neck
or tattooed on the face of a cuckoo clock.

Because numerals occur in tinned spaghetti
I continue to sing in the morning.

Everyday I drown numerals in bathwater
and when I left my country

I smuggled numerals in my shoes.

Fibrous structure

We always strive to contain the soft stuff yet
    Magdalena Abakanowicz weaves herself into her Abakans
        not to hide of course   though that would be easy to do
          but to   burst out   and discharge
            the tension   she's built up in them.

We might recall the big fibrous vaginal one
    hanging red   in outer space
       the experimental music or the woman in the distance
          moving along the sand dunes.

Choosing softness comes out of a need to protest
  she's quite clear and borders
    are full of smells sisal and horsehair
      but there's also the chafe
        of old ropes thrown in.

Though I know the word *contain*
  can entertain *restrain someone* or *control oneself*
    its root *ten* holds me both
      tender and in tension.

Yesterday I found you hiding   behind the radiator.
  I don't know how long you'd been there
    but judging by the dust on you I said oh dad
      why didn't I know what you were hiding?
        You stared half-smiling against the blue.

Ultimately your heart is a thumping machine
  tan belt and whack and whether you like it or not
    rage contains   rag and age
      which just about sums you up.

Inside a microwave an egg will explode
  but a lightbulb in water will brighten
    and contain
      its own light.

Do you remember the chestbuster scene in *Alien*
  or the facehugger
      injecting into its host a tiny egg
       whose enzymes slowly soften
        the tissues around the sternum?

I said dad I'm guilty it was me
  but I've slit it here and here and here
    and look the rag-rage of us
      discharging softly.

Jay-Philippe Vibert

dawn
(from 'basilisk', Chapter Four)

helices chatter

(Beilstein rewrites Beilstein

    profligate mark at the molecular)

a breath of life

(of course, ours is a science taught by constellations,

    even the stars can sense the enormity of our uniqueness)

beginning

(Darwin blushed to theorize a peacock tail)

an engine stops in electric shock

bursting the frailty of its fumes

a narwhal shrieking at the surface lay

dives disturbed

cars lub roadside in plush alarum

spiders web, luminesce and brook

sugary fronds, slow-dripping saliva

flicker, vanish

a salamander's tail and tongue

our road divides,

the spine undulates drenches of tarmac

drills skewer the air petrified roar of crystal

cranes gob steel

                lassoes

    in time

helices chatter

pigeons crowd a crust

like screens of bristling

angels clustering a saint

as a cat licks at a puddle

whiskers rinsed in rainbows

working on the in-breath

    brachiates

coral   to   clinker

a crab falls forward with the swell

waving red anemones on blue claws

the pursuit is not for a reflection but the pursuit itself

there is no magic but in the telling

'spellbound' is merely accurate

at fault, paradigms

a bluff in this expanse

impulse teratogenic

wasps gather   a crushed snail's ichor

now

    there are no lines for justification to cross

    but the point is before extinction

try

    there is no act beyond your own

    choke. The tongue is brittle &

    hopeful, is jaunty, dissolves

Margaret Ann Wadleigh

Beguiled by the Gyre

Chartres' spires rumble up from the crypt,
the place of her pangs. Underearth, a Celtic

well remains, a dark portal of shut-eyed
blankness, unwishing. Once, folk on foot

encircled thrice, to conjure the guardian
sprite of the spring: their Underground Lady:

Notre Dame Sous Terre. Shards of limestone,
relics of cemented bones disguise the fluids

in soil. Today, from a driveway a purple
violet clambers up a tiny crag of concrete,

climbing its local crevice in dank Spring
to pose (to solve) the Paschal Mystery,

to recall that there were other labors: eons
and eons of contractions, travails, volcanic

spasms and titanic shifts that transformed
ocean beds into sky-steeples of snow.

The ancestors said that God was unhappy
because it thundered on Easter Day

and yet, now, in the Himalayas, pilgrims
find seashells on the peaks: the ammonite

coils ascend and descend, always making
still, headway on a timeline of vertigo.

Atmosphere

It seemed to me that I beheld a beauteous tree
uplifted in the air. —Dream of the Rood

On campus, a groundskeeper drives a stake
near a tree to hold a plaque. The old wooden
mallet strikes, but as if to raise an objection
—jolts— to say: stop! something's here. Below
in the dark, pachyderm herds of roots meander—
tail to trunk, tail to trunk, connecting an elder
matron ash, to infant sprouts. It is— for them
that she sips up rivulets of groundwater
and thwarts its descent to the sea. For them—
she extracts hydrogen in her sungreen crown.
For them, she devours, sighs: carbon to oxygen:
photons to breath. Soon the mallet will affix
our Ash's sinews to a college chancellor's name
in ever-blooming bronze. Do trees, though, name
themselves? Do they scheme ways to etch those
names, on us, inhalers of air? Or, perhaps?
inscribe a brass plaque: "Homo sapiens! We make
clouds." Do remind me: not to forget our debt.

Honey in the Rock

After Psalm 34:8

I observe in stone the remains of a cataclysm,
so, naturally Emeril Lagasse: the Louisiana chef
comes to mind. Here, the Fossiliferous Limestone
suggests fragrant lime and calcium carbonate
combined by a deft force, so as not to overwhelm
the pasta-twisting coral colony. I see: *finalissima!*
how diatom algae were tossed on sizzling rock—
a theatrical garnish—*bam!*— for the camera.

Lord knows we taste with our eyes, David saith.
O! taste and see, the Lord is good. . . he preserves
all his bones, and flesh, for a holy transformation.
Look there—on this stone's surface: scallop shells,
concave and convex, all set out for a future buffet—
but for now— bleached pink bowls brim with rain.

Isobel Armstrong

from Broken Glass

3 Fight — remembering Keats

all it takes

blood and glass
a quarrel in the street
a broken bottle
jagged edge
a cry
aortic blood
pulmonary red
too literal
to be imagined
bleeding to death
in five minutes

but once understanding
his own lungs how glass
blushed with blood
that impossible red
incarnadine   vermilion
fused in light and glass
that
red ichor where
saints and apostles jostle
for place in high windows
blessed with redness
plasma of glass robes and
angel wings and doves
redness that intensest
  no

words   vermilion
ruby scarlet carmine cinnabar
except when
twilight stains   cast
a radiance on a cathedral's stone floor
remembering red
remembrance
imagining

4 Crystal

'It was as if a fracture in delicate crystal had begun'.
George Eliot. *Middlemarch*, Lydgate's marriage.

fissure
invisible   almost

a fissure in crystal though
the split sides cleave
as if
as if
parting   asunder
the breach rhymes itself
as if
assuaging an
originary rupture though

intransigent crystal
incorporates
an almost invisible
dyad
in its lustre
striation
two lines
held apart
in the tense glass

Mark Ward

Low Ceilings
after Larkin

All my friends have done away with lust:
a scarf they left behind and do not miss.
I sit outside an interchangeable
bar, watch young men commit to the premise:

someone'll always find them attractive.
It's in the eyes, I tell the empty chair,
imagining you captivated.
We watch heads turn, eyes meet, that knowing stare

focussed on me, for a moment, and he's gone,
content to look and move on with his night.
That's not right, Phillip says, lighting a smoke.

All I have is bitterness, he half-jokes.
He drags me up, throws me towards the throng.
The man looks again. In his eyes, I see life.

Latent

I slept all morning
and most of the afternoon.
In July discomfort,
the energy leaked from me,
piggybacking upon my sweat.

Walking with this heavy body,
there's a helpless swaying
like Godzilla after the final blow
but before he collapses into
the building full of screams.

I lie on my broken sofa, beached.
The day continuing to provide
for those who meet it. I could
shower and head out. I could
get up and stop this succumbing.

I can do anything; a lie to hold
the darkness captive. Keep distracted.
Sometimes the world is softer than
I remember. A lightness, a breeze,
the sun catching on the branches.

Today I wish for that selflessness,
a cupped hand, a smile but that's not
what's outside, there's a slick veneer of care,
a welcoming at one's own risk. The world's
understandable selfishness. The door

remains closed. I've gone back to
bed, writing today off completely.
These planless afternoons, full of
possibilities, are muted light fading.
There is still time, I write, underlining it.

Janet Sutherland

from The True Briton, an N.F.S.Q. Barque of 1046 tons

(extracts from the journal of Victor E. Smyth made on a voyage to Australia with Geraldine & Julian Smyth 1875–76)

28th Dec. 1875: At 12 O'clock noon we were exactly under the sun, we stuck penknives upright in the deck & there was no shadow. V E S

I have set my knife
in the body of the ship
and eaten all darkness
where are the shadows of war
where are the shadows on the lung

4th Jan. 1876: Sighted a vessel said to be the Lammermoor of the 19th ult. Dancing on the poop in the evening. I dressed in female clothes & caused amusement. T. Scarth played the fiddle. V E S

My father   who would often work in shorts
bare chested   bringing hay bales in
took me aside one hot day in July
the year I turned eleven   my chest
must now be covered-up   I could
not walk the fields like him   though
no one else would see   My childish skin
scribbled by cut-stemmed summer
grasses   laved by air which licked
me with its tongue   would be
incarcerated   bound   what is shame?
what is rage?   I learned that day
the simplest forms of them

2nd Feb 1876: Cook threw his white dog overboard, being out of its depth it was drowned. V E S

lured in as witnesses and connoisseurs
our diarist denies us extra notes
offers the germs of war and genocide

11th July 1876: At 1pm Mr H returns, and we dine. The most startling feature about this meal is that nothing is drunk but tea. I always ask for a glass of water. V E S

So that dragonflies may flick and dart
so that they buzz and creak
until the tongue asks for water
for something to swallow
so that cattle may drink
that they may toss their heads
cast droplets back along their flanks
until the mouth researches
runnels and channels
so that kingfishers may flash
and fish idle in the shallows

Norman Jope

From the Westernmost Bridge

Shelley in Pisa

The young man surveys the sunset, its darkest barriers of cinereous cloud—his death lies in that direction, beyond the Arno's mouth, but even if visible it can't be expressed in words. The silence of the Mediterranean depths has no equivalent in the streak of dun and sulphureous gold that lingers overhead like a newly-made scar. No sight on earth can summon the reality of death... for where it is, we are not. We can only summon its likeness in the things of earth. He cannot finish the poem... he has two years of experience to cram in at lightning speed before the boat overturns and his spirit sinks into the waters. He ends it with the word Gold and returns to his palatial lodgings and infatuations—lets life pile in, for he must drink it up as quickly as he can. That sunset has told him all he knows, and all that he will need to know. A quiet half-unpeopled town is his to feel at home in for the briefest of interludes... I resurrect him briefly as a wrinkled image, trembling and unfading on the city's westernmost bridge.

Thury's Shoals

We're in the gallery's basement, watched by globular fish-men who ooze from the walls—trying too hard to steal our souls, they stare at us blankly in a barrage of anonymous browns. Some are headless and have faces in their navels. Some are faces adorned by infinitesimal insect wings. Others are lumps of cosmic ectoplasm, waiting—almost certainly in vain—for the shem to be placed in their mouths.

These Gigeresque babies are insatiable for the life that we convey, even in December's premature dusks, and open their mouths as if to plead. We deny them, passing from one construction to another, evading the pale blue pencil that is held in one of their mouths but which will never scrawl a word of sense. The Will's compulsion to survive, in no matter what distorted form, reminds us that we are no less benighted.

We're passing through a cellar in the Prague of Ripellino or Meyrink, stared at with envy and beseeching, as if we might become the vehicles of their escape… risking the alarms to tear them down from the walls and carry them up the stairs into the dankness of dusk, so that we see them ooze and scuttle down the streets of their adopted home.

It's the eyes that distract us most of all, even more so than the mouths. The mouths convey a certain longing… but the eyes express the combined curiosity and stupidity of the newly-born, a Will to exist that mystifies itself and has no words with which to express its mystification. Nor any rabbi to cajole it into life or return it to the nightside of the star-strewn tree.

Raising its two striped hands, the King of the Golems stares from the depths of its interior void and silently announces the cessation of time, the conclusion of all thought and hope and love. We are seduced content… we have nothing more to say.

Levente Thury (1941–2007), Hungarian sculptor and ceramic artist of Jewish heritage, allegedly descended from Rabbi Loew. The exhibition took place at the Műcsarnok, Budapest in December 2021.

Three Wise Birds

I didn't hide in the Dunwich museum on that summer night, so failed to witness the escape of the heron, the bittern and the spoonbill. I'd wanted them to smash their sad glass cases and fly off past the painstaking reconstruction of the underwater city, the Ship Inn and the tidy row of cottages, in the direction of Walberswick and the swaying reeds of Corporation, Westwood or Dingle Marshes.

So, whilst I slept a fitful sleep in a bed and breakfast in Lowestoft, the trio summoned the will to smash those cases to pieces, evade those labels, escape the prison of their pasts and the arrogance of their assassins... shaking broken glass from their wings, they marched down the staircase and the heron picked the lock with its beak. Past the leper hospital and St James' Farm, to the right of Dunwich Forest they stalked until they reached the windmill.

There was black-green flatness under glossy summer sky moth-riddled with stars... the North Sea's silence barely rippling with the bells of the city swaddled beneath it. There were reeds in which they could hide once more and build their nests, regaining lives that had been taken from them for the sake of sport and enlightenment—sentient creatures that had owed us nothing but had nonetheless paid their debt.

If I were to return one summer night and rummage through the reeds, going deeper in and further from my life, I am sure that I would find them once more... heron first, then spoonbill, then bittern as befitting their rareness. I'd apologise to each in turn for the violence of my species, in the hope of the briefest wing-tip brushed against the palm of my hand, and would never be seen or heard of again until I flew out over the North Sea's expanse—no longer remembering my name or the mission that had brought me back to these shores.

Giles Goodland

Illumination

Beyond the realm of bird circle floats from a face, places its lips on me. Scales of rain fall from my eyes when I look into it. In the quarter light of the moon listen. God's silence contains the sum of all noise. Our first language was light, followed by the sound echoing, not echoing through the public domain. Time hurtles, wind carries delicate sentence-structures. They sway and nod.

Departure

Cars tut under the forest's drum pressure. Like at the start of a beautiful war film, the birds are leaving. Geese's sonar. The trees smudge up a prayer which the wind drives off.

Alphabet

The devil's work is before this. Without it we would store the world in sense order. In the war against names I am on the side which holds denotation fails discourse, but the lark sleeps under my hand. Trees print a list of birds which the sky files daily into its unmarked cabinet.

Honour

The cloven beard turns on the blinded wheel, offices fill reservoirs with hair. This has no attachment at all to the things that are, interacting without knowing where dogmatic procedures drown. Poems intruded upon him like burglars, themselves of unsmooth mind.

Empiricism

In the way a stone happens, a sentence. The bewildered climbed from their ethers onto grass-like biers. Look up at me as I climb into the loft. My feet sump. Spirit is a virus, the slumbrous masses think thought has no shape. Their belief hardens. What remains to be destroyed? What was never there, the ever inside it.

Notes on Contributors

Rizwan Akhtar's debut collection of poems *Lahore, I Am Coming* (2017) was published by Punjab University Press. He works as an Assistant Professor in the Department of English, Punjab University, Lahore. His poetry has been published in magazines in the UK, USA, India, Canada, and New Zealand.

Isobel Armstrong is emeritus professor of English at Birkbeck, University of London and a senior research fellow of the Institute of English Studies at the University of London. She has published widely on Victorian poetry. Her own poetry publications include *Reveries of Glass* (Sparrow Press, 2019).

Jack Barron teaches at the University of Cambridge, and has a PhD on the work of W. S. Graham. His creative and critical work has appeared in *Cambridge Quarterly, PN Review, Burlington Contemporary, Review, Critical Quarterly*, and elsewhere.

Leia K. Bradley (they/she) is a backwoods Georgia born, Brooklyn based lesbian writer, performance artist and an MFA Poetry candidate at Columbia University, where she also teaches Writing in Gender & Sexuality. She has work out now or forthcoming in *Poetry Magazine, Variant, Nimrod, Aurore, Ghost City, JMWW, trampset, Wild Greens, Peach Fuzz, Full House Literary, West Trade Review*, and more, with her poem 'Settle(d)' chosen as the Editor's Choice Best Overall pick for *Penumbra Magazine*'s 2022 Pride issue. She was nominated by *Miniskirt Magazine* for a Pushcart Prize for her lesbian werewolf short story "Moon Pie," and is the 2023 Featured Author of *Anodyne Magazine*. Twitter @LeiaKBradley; instagram @MadameMort.

Tom Cowin has published two pamphlets, with Broken Sleep and Red Ceilings Press. Work has also appeared in *Tears in the Fence, Stride, Datableed* and *Morphrog*. He is a support worker for the homeless, and a gardener.

Claire Crowther has several books from Shearsman, with a New and Selected volume, *Real Lear*, due later in 2024, alongside a collection of her essays.

Katy Evans-Bush is a poet, essayist and blogger, and lives in Kent, where she is a freelance poetry tutor and editor. Her new poetry collection, *Joe Hill Makes His Way into the Castle*, is published by CB Editions.

Mark Fiddes lives in the Middle East. His second collection, *Other Saints Are Available*, was published in 2022 by Live Canon. Poems have recently appeared in *Oxford Poetry, The Irish Times, The Brixton Review of Books, The Forward Book of Poetry, Magma, Stand* and *The North*. He is a winner of the Oxford Brookes University International Prize, the Westport Festival Prize and the Ruskin Prize as well as being a runner up in the Bridport Prize and the National Poetry Competition. He's currently translating the work of Catalan poet Miquel Martí i Pol.

Giles Goodland has two collections from Shearsman Books, most recently *The Masses*. Others have appeared from Salt, KFS and Free Verse Editions/Parlor Press, which issued his most recent collection, *Civil Twilight*.

Sylee Gore is an artist, poet, and translator.

Ellen Harrold started publishing her poetry a year ago and chalked up ten magazine appearances in 2023. She has also been reviewing for *Dundee University Review of the Arts* (DURA). She lives in Scotland.

Jill Jones' latest book is *Acrobat Music: New and Selected Poems* (Puncher & Wattmann, Waratah, NSW, 2023). Other recent books include *Wild Curious Air* and *A History of What I'll Become*. Her work has appeared in *Arc, Blackbox Manifold, Jacket2, The Manchester Review, Meanjin, Poetry, Poetry Review, Shearsman, Softblow, The Stinging Fly, takahe* and other periodicals in Australia, Canada, Ireland, New Zealand, Singapore, Sweden, UK, and USA.

Norman Jope has two collections from Shearsman, including *The Rest of the World* (2021) and two from Waterloo Press. A new volume, *Lands of Lost Content*, has just been published by Waterloo Press. He lives in Plymouth.

Karin Lessing is an expatriate American poet living in Provence for many years. Shearsman Books published her *Collected Poems* in 2010.

Bernadette McCarthy Flahive is from Cork. Her chapbook *Bog Arabic* was published by Southword Editions (2018). Her work has appeared in journals including *Acumen, Agenda, Crannóg, The London Magazine, Poetry Ireland Review,* and *Southword,* as well as in *Poetry International 25/26* (San Diego University Press, 2019).

Katherine Meehan is a writer from North Carolina. Her work has appeared in *Magma, The Kenyon Review, Bath Magg, Anthropocene,* and other journals. Her first collection, *Dame Julie Andrews' Botched Vocal Cord Surgery*, has just been published with Two Rivers Press. She is a co-organiser of Reading's Poets' Café and is currently researching tarot card ekphrasis for a practice-based PhD.

David Miller was born in Melbourne, Australia, but has lived in the UK for many years. His more recent publications include *Reassembling Still: Collected Poems* (Shearsman Books, 2014), *Spiritual Letters* (Contraband Books, 2017 / Spuyten Duyvil, 2022), *Towards a Menagerie* (Chax Press, 2019), *Matrix I & II* (Guillemot Press, 2020), *Some Other Days and Nights* (above/ground press, 2021), *Afterword* (Shearsman Books, 2022), *circle square triangle* (Spuyten Duyvil, 2022), *An Envelope for Silence* (above/ground press, 2022), *Some Other Shadows* (Knives Forks and Spoons Press, 2022) and *Time, Wisdom and Koalas* (Chax Press, 2023). He is also a painter and a musician.

At the time of her death, aged 22, in 2014, **Sophia Nugent-Siegal** was a postgraduate student in ancient history at Macquarie University, Sydney, from which she also held a undergraduate degree in ancient history. She was a poet and an emerging author of speculative-fiction. Periods of her youth had been spent in Italy and England, which influenced her work and study. Her poetry collection, *Oracle*, was published in 2007, when she was 16. The poem printed here is previously unpublished, and is the last poem that she wrote.

Joseph Nutman is a poet from North Hertfordshire who finds his voice in the tension between nature, society, and the psyche. He made it to the longlist of The Plaza Audio Poetry Prize, and has had poems featured by *Spelt, Poetry Cove,* and *IS&T*.

Ann Pelletier-Topping is originally from Montreal, and works as a French teacher in Devon. She won second prize in the National Poetry Competition, was longlisted in the Fish Poetry and the Rebecca Swift Foundation Women Poets' Prizes and her work has appeared in *Ambit, Poetry Review, Tears in the Fence* and *Obsessed with Pipework*.

Janet Sutherland's fifth Shearsman volume, *The Messenger House*, was published in 2023.

Helen Tookey is based in Liverpool. She writes poems and short prose and has collaborated with musicians Sharron Kraus and Martin Heslop. She has published three poetry collections with Carcanet, *Missel-Child* (2014), *City of Departures* (2019), and *In the Quaker Hotel* (2022).

Jay-Philippe Vibert works in tech engineering—software/hardware/research. He says that "'basilisk' is an attempt to find a scientific lyrical language and talk about nature, cities, fossil fuels, immersion, vision: an impossible attempt at reflection".

Margaret Ann Wadleigh lives in Norman, Oklahoma. Her work has appeared previously in *Shearsman* (Nᵒ 131 & 132), and in *Image Journal* (Issue 113).

Mark Ward has a full-length collection *Nightlight* (Salmon Poetry, 2023) and four chapbooks: *Circumference* (Finishing Line Press, 2018), *Carcass* (Seven Kitchens Press, 2020), *HIKE* (Bear Creek Press, 2022), and the online Choose Your Own Adventure sonnet, *Faultline* (voidspace, 2022). He lives in Dublin.

Alex Wong has published two collections with Carcanet, *Poems Without Irony* (2017) and *Shadow and Refrain* (2021). His poems and translations have appeared in a number of journals, including *Bad Lilies, Butcher's Dog, Cyphers, The Fortnightly Review, Inventory, Long Poem Magazine, Modern Poetry in Translation, PN Review* and *Stand*. For Carcanet Classics he has edited volumes of Swinburne and Pater.

Milton Keynes UK
Ingram Content Group UK Ltd.
UKHW031527120324
439228UK00001B/40